BATS

LIVING WILD

LIVING WILD

Published by Creative Paperbacks
P.O. Box 227, Mankato, Minnesota 56002
Creative Paperbacks is an imprint of The Creative Company
www.thecreativecompany.us

Design and production by Mary Herrmann
Art direction by Rita Marshall
Printed by Corporate Graphics in the United States of America

Photographs by 123RF (Todd Arena, Matt Caldwell), Alamy (Avico Ltd, Danita Delmont, Robert Fried, John Mitchell, Rolf Nussbaumer, Papilio, Gerry Pearce, Peter Arnold, Inc., Sternwarte-Weinheim, Krystyna Szulecka), Corbis (Visuals Unlimited), Dreamstime (Michiel Bosch, Steve Byland, Jaroslaw Domanski, Terrance Emerson, Freeze, Grigory Kubatyan, Michael Lynch, Charles Outcalt, Luis Santos, Tolitsayala, Dariusz Wiejaczka, Worldfoto), Getty Images (Bruce Dale/National Geographic, Tim Flach, Lynn Johnson/ National Geographic, Mattias Klum), Paul Heideman, iStockphoto (Chris Brown, George Burba, Chris Burt, Craig Dingle, Donald Gargano, Tom Grundy, Michelle Hamel, Samuel Jolly, Serge Leguevacques, Michael Lynch, Pamela Moore, James Nader, Nicholas Rjabow, Michael Rolands)

The Library of Congress has cataloged the hardcover edition as follows:
Gish, Melissa.
Bats / by Melissa Gish.
p. cm. — (Living wild)
Includes bibliographical references and index.
Summary: A look at bats, including their habitats, physical characteristics such as their fragile wings, behaviors, relationships with humans, and persecuted status in the world today.
ISBN 978-1-58341-966-3 (hardcover)
ISBN 978-0-89812-549-8 (pbk)
1. Bats—Juvenile literature. I. Title. II. Series.

QL737.C5G56 2010
599.4—dc22   2009025167

CPSIA: 012411 PO1420

9 8 7 6 5 4 3 2

CREATIVE
PAPER BACKS

BATS
Melissa Gish

Far above ground, the topmost
leaves of a tall eucalyptus tree shiver

as a slender, leathery figure hanging
from a high branch begins to move.

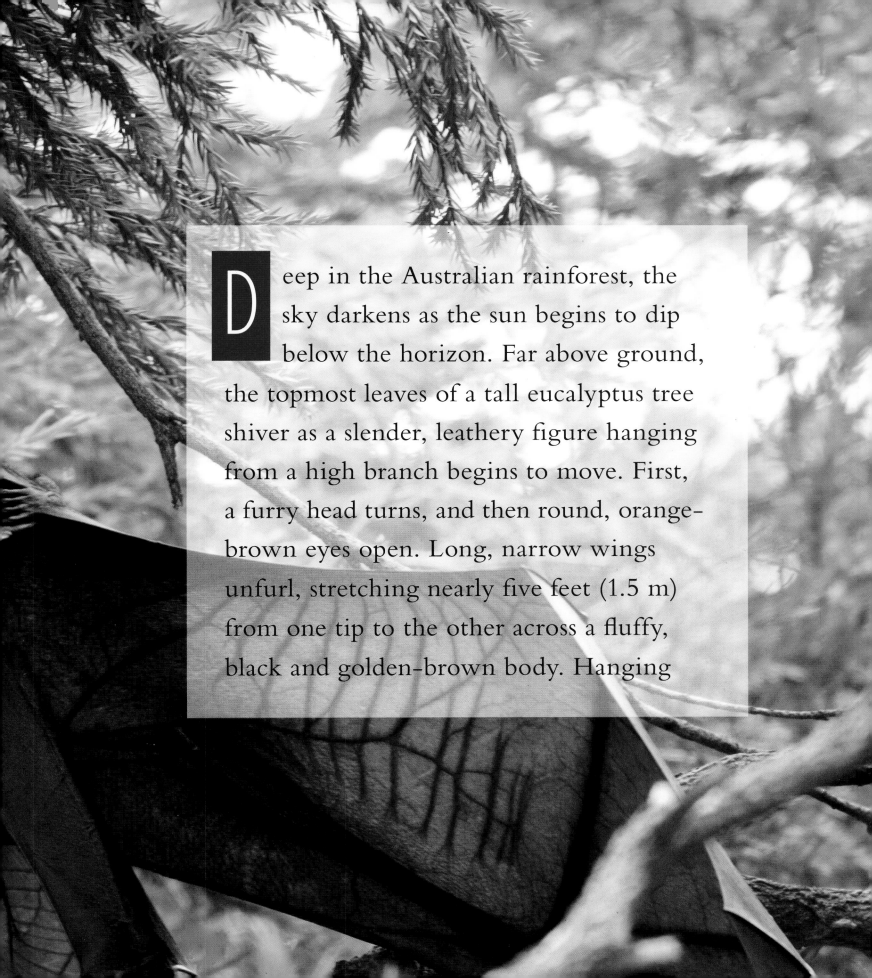

D eep in the Australian rainforest, the sky darkens as the sun begins to dip below the horizon. Far above ground, the topmost leaves of a tall eucalyptus tree shiver as a slender, leathery figure hanging from a high branch begins to move. First, a furry head turns, and then round, orange-brown eyes open. Long, narrow wings unfurl, stretching nearly five feet (1.5 m) from one tip to the other across a fluffy, black and golden-brown body. Hanging

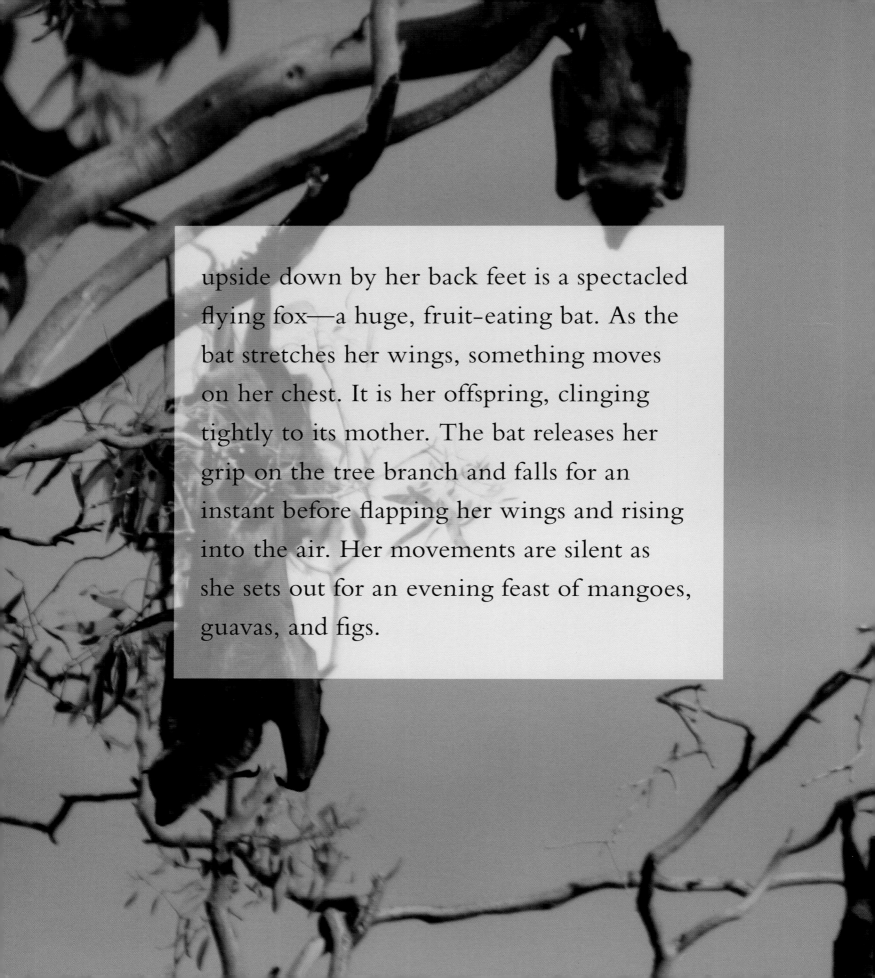

upside down by her back feet is a spectacled flying fox—a huge, fruit-eating bat. As the bat stretches her wings, something moves on her chest. It is her offspring, clinging tightly to its mother. The bat releases her grip on the tree branch and falls for an instant before flapping her wings and rising into the air. Her movements are silent as she sets out for an evening feast of mangoes, guavas, and figs.

WHERE IN THE WORLD THEY LIVE

Vampire Bat
from Mexico
south to Brazil

African straw-colored Fruit Bat
Botswana

Ghost Bat
northern
Australia

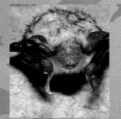

Large or Great Mouse-eared Bat
Europe

Malayan Flying Fox
Southeast Asia,
particularly
Malaysia and
Myanmar

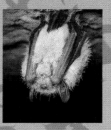

Eastern Pipistrelle
eastern half of
North America
as far north as
Ontario, Central
America as far
south as Honduras

Brown long-eared Bat
across northern
Europe and
Asia, from Great
Britain to Japan

Sac-winged Bat
tropical regions
worldwide

Barbastelle Bat
southern
England and
Wales, western
Europe

Numbering some 1,000 species, bats can be
found throughout the world as far north as
the Arctic but not as far south as Antarctica.
While the great majority of bats live in tropical
regions, others live in North America, Europe,
and several places in the Northern Hemisphere.
The colored squares represent some common
locations of nine bat species.

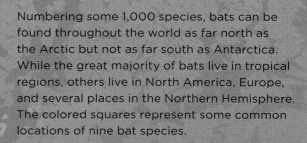

FURRY FLIERS

Tropical bats are built to cope with tick infestations and upset stomachs that come from eating unripe fruit.

Today, there are more than 5,000 species of mammals on Earth. About 1,000 of these are bats, the only flying mammals. Bats make up a unique order of animals called Chiroptera, meaning "hand-wing," and are divided into two suborders: Megachiroptera (megabats) and Microchiroptera (microbats). Only 46 species of bat are found in North America. The others are scattered throughout the rest of the world, mostly in tropical regions, but some in the Arctic as well. None are found in Antarctica.

Bats, like all mammals, are warm-blooded. This means they are able to keep their body temperature at a constant level, no matter what the temperature is outside. Mammals may adjust their body temperatures by sweating to cool down or shivering to warm up. Some mammals, including a number of bat species, even **hibernate** in cold weather. All bat mothers give birth to live young (as opposed to laying eggs) and produce milk to feed them.

The closest modern relatives of bats are **primates**. The bones in a bat's wing are similar to the bones in a human's

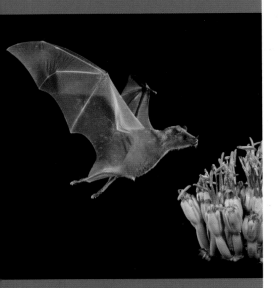

The lesser long-nosed bat feeds mainly on nectar in the southern U.S. and Mexico.

As it laps **nectar** from flowers, the Pallas's long-tongued bat flaps its wings downward, creating a whirlwind that holds the bat's body aloft.

arm and hand. But the bat's four finger bones are long and connected by two layers of skin that form a wing. The wing runs the length of the bat's body and attaches to the hind leg. The two hind legs of most bats are connected by a **membrane** called a uropatagium (*yoo-roh-puh-TAY-jee-um*). Some bat species have a tail attached to this membrane as well. Most tails are short, but the three species of mouse-tailed bat have tails as long as their head and body put together.

Since strong muscles are needed for flight, a bat's chest and shoulders are the strongest parts of its body. The rear of a bat's body is small, and its hind feet are short, with sharp claws designed to help the bat cling to surfaces as it roosts, or settles in to sleep. All but one species of megabat also have a claw on the second finger that is used to grip fruit, the main food source of these bats.

All bats have soft fur covering their bodies but not their wings. Fur varies in color, from the pale golden hammerhead bat to the bright orange leaf-nosed bat to the black flying fox. Bats also vary in size. The smallest in the world is the Philippine bamboo bat (also known as the bumblebee bat). This bat is only 1.5 inches (3.8 cm) long

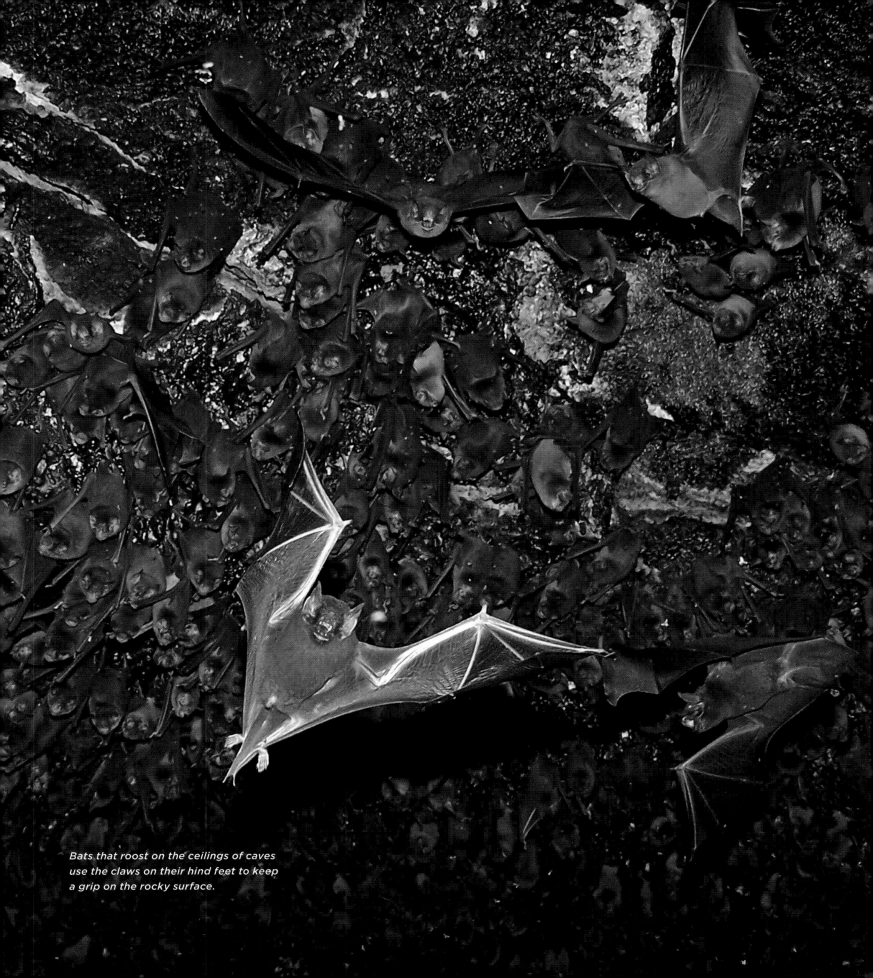

Bats that roost on the ceilings of caves use the claws on their hind feet to keep a grip on the rocky surface.

A vampire bat feeds on the blood of farm animals, birds, and even seals for about 30 minutes at a time.

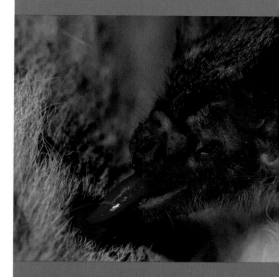

and weighs just 0.05 ounce (1.4 g)—about the weight of a dime. The world's largest bat is the giant golden-crowned fruit bat, which weighs up to three pounds (1.4 kg) and has a wingspan of more than five feet (1.5 m). With a wingspan of 22 inches (56 cm), the largest bat in North America is the greater mastiff bat.

Different bats have different food sources. Three microbat species feed only on blood. These vampire bats are found throughout Mexico and Central and South America. The common vampire bat preys mainly on farm animals, while hairy-legged and white-winged vampire bats prey on birds. A vampire bat uses its sharp teeth to make tiny cuts in the skin of its prey. Substances in the bat's saliva keep the victim's blood flowing while the bat laps up the blood with its tongue. One ounce (28.3 g) of blood is often enough to satisfy a vampire bat for two or three days, and the victim is usually left alive.

Some megabats eat nectar and **pollen**. There are more than 150 species of megabat, which, because of their diet, are important **pollinators** and seed spreaders. In fact, at least 95 percent of the regrowth in rainforests is credited to bats that deposit seeds in their droppings as they fly.

Vampire bats are the only mammals with heat-sensing organs—pits around the nose leaves that detect the skin temperature of prey.

Short-tailed fruit bats have sharp teeth, enabling them to separate the juice from the pulp of the fruit when feeding.

Megabats rely on their vision to find food, so they have large eyes that help them see at night. Most megabats can also see in color, which helps them determine which fruits are ripe and which flowers are filled with pollen. Most flowers pollinated by bats are pale in color and stand out against the darkness.

Microbats rely on **echolocation** rather than vision to maneuver in flight and capture the insects that make up their diet. These bats have smaller eyes and larger ears than megabats. A single bat can snatch between 600 and 1,000 mosquitoes and other insects in just an hour. Some microbats also eat frogs, birds, fish, and even other bats. Unlike most other bats, some bats such as the New Zealand lesser short-tailed bat eat both fruit and insects; this rare species crawls on the ground to find food.

Certain facial features help differentiate between—and provide names for—bat species. Some microbats have fleshy leaf-shaped structures on their faces called nose leaves. Scientists believe the nose leaves help bats direct their echolocation signals, which are sent through their noses. The greater spear-nosed bat has long, spear-shaped nose

Flying foxes learn to fly at about three months of age and are ready to find food.

Jamaican fruit bats will travel six to nine miles (9.7–14.5 km) around their Central and South American habitats to find food.

Zoos and animal sanctuaries obtain special permits to house their own bat colonies.

About 750,000 Mexican free-tailed bats live in the world's largest urban bat colony, located in the city of Austin, Texas.

leaves, while the wrinkle-faced bat has stout nose leaves that look like crumpled paper. The greater horseshoe bat is named for its horseshoe-shaped nose leaves.

Some microbats, such as the big brown bat, send their echolocation signals through their mouths. Big brown bats and hoary bats are the only two kinds of bats whose signals can be heard by humans. The echolocation signals of other bats are too high-pitched for human hearing to detect. Bats are not the only animals that use echolocation. Dolphins, toothed whales, porpoises, and some kinds of birds and shrews also echolocate.

Bats' echolocation system is 1,000 times more powerful than similar human technology, such as the sonar used by submarines. To echolocate, bats send out pulses of high-frequency sound that hit objects in their path. These sound pulses bounce back, like echoes, and the bats can detect the location and size of objects around them. The objects can be as big as a rock or a tree, or they can be as small as a mosquito. A bat's ability to echolocate is so acute—and its flying skill so precise—that it can avoid colliding with an object as slender as a human hair—even in complete darkness.

Little brown bats, some of the most abundant bats in North America, echolocate to find their insect prey.

Bats like caves because temperatures remain relatively constant, usually between 50 and 60 °F (10 to 15.5 °C).

JUST HANGING OUT

Bats are nocturnal animals, meaning they are active at night instead of during the day. In the daytime, bats gather together to roost upside down in trees, caves, and cliffs. A group of bats is called a colony. Bats are most at risk from predators—owls, hawks, snakes, and, in some cases, larger bats—when they are resting, but their protected roosts help them stay **camouflaged**, and when they leave their roosts to look for food, they keep on the move.

Most bat species cannot fly from a grounded position; instead, they must drop from above. When on the ground, a bat's sharp claws allow it to climb up trees and rocks to gain a better position for takeoff. Bat species have different flight styles according to their body type. Bats with small bodies and large, broad wings fly slowly but maneuver well to chase and capture darting insects. About 70 percent of bat species are built to instantly adjust their flight movements and shift directions while in pursuit of prey.

Some bats with broad wings can hover. This allows them to feed on nectar or pollen in much the same way as a hummingbird does. Apart from hummingbirds and a few insects, no other creatures are capable of this sort of

Rust-colored eastern red bats often hang by one foot to resemble dead leaves and change roosts often to avoid detection by predatory birds.

wing movement. Bats with large bodies and long, narrow wings can fly swiftly but are less maneuverable. These bats may journey long distances as they forage for food.

In the winter, entire bat colonies may enter a long-term state of inactivity, called hibernation, or they may migrate to warmer climates. Some bats, such as eastern red bats, roost alone. Red bats that live in the southern United States often do not need to migrate because winters are not as severe. Still, they conserve their body heat during colder

times by spending part of the day in a short-term state of torpor, which means their body functions and **metabolism** slow down. At night, the solitary bats become active again. In tropical regions, bats neither migrate nor hibernate.

Colonies may contain a dozen or fewer members, but most contain many more. Carlsbad Caverns National Park in New Mexico is the summer home of about 400,000 Mexican free-tailed bats. Bracken Cave, in Texas, is home to many more of the species—around 20 million.

Tourists gather at the Congress Avenue Bridge in Austin, Texas, to watch bats emerge from their roosts.

Bats that feed on fruit and nectar have long tongues, while small insect-eating bats have short tongues.

Almost all bat species communicate with one another by making vocal clicks and whistles that humans can hear. Bats also make scent markings by secreting an odorous liquid from scent glands near their faces or wings, and they may use body movements and aerial maneuvers to communicate as well. Bats use these methods of communication to identify and attract one another, especially during mating season.

The climate in which bats live often determines the timing of their breeding season. The reason for this is so the young will be born into a time of abundant food sources. Cold-weather bats usually mate in autumn before they hibernate, but offspring do not begin to develop inside their mothers until early spring. Many tropical bats breed according to their habitats' cycles of rainy and dry seasons, and some species can have two breeding periods per year.

Some species, such as the little brown bat, mate randomly within the colony. For other species, including the sac-winged bat, courtship is a complex process that involves making scent marks and singing special songs. The males of species such as the white-lined bat gather groups of females together and defend them against other males as part of courtship, too.

Gestation varies by species and takes anywhere from 40 days to 6 months. Baby bats, called pups, are born feet first, which is unusual for mammals. The mother bat hangs from a roost using the claws on her wings and curls her feet and tail membrane up to create a scoop, which catches the baby as it is born. The pup then instinctively crawls up its mother's belly and clings tightly to her chest, feeding on the milk she produces.

Most female bats have one pup per year. Several species, such as the eastern pipistrelle, have twins, and only a few bat species can produce more than two offspring at a time. Red bats, which typically give birth to three or four young, are the only bats whose females have four nipples, enabling up to four pups to feed at once. All other bats have just two nipples. Such a small litter size causes bats to be some of the slowest reproducing animals on Earth.

Depending on the species, newborn bat pups weigh between 10 and 35 percent of their mother's weight. For example, an adult big brown bat weighs .8 ounce (23 g) and typically gives birth to twins, each weighing .14 ounce (4 g), for a total of about one-third of her weight. Microbats are born blind and hairless, while megabats

Some fruit bats have extra claws on each foot to enable them to cling tightly to tree bark.

Tropical bats that eat frogs can determine which frogs are poisonous by listening to the sounds of the frogs' mating calls.

Microbat species that are born hairless become miniature versions of their parents once their fur grows in.

are born furry and with their eyes open. All pups depend on their mothers for nourishing milk and security. The females of most bat species are the primary caregivers, but a few species, such as the African yellow-winged bat and the Papillose woolly bat of Asia, live in family groups, and fathers help care for the young.

Some mother bats carry their young when they hunt, while others leave them clinging to cave walls or in the care of a bat "babysitter." When the mother returns to the colony, she can identify her offspring by its unique vocal sounds and scent. Growth varies by species but is generally rapid. Most bats begin to fly by two to four weeks of age and stop feeding on their mothers' milk shortly thereafter, when they become self-sufficient.

In the world of mammals, the general rule is that larger animals have longer life spans. For example, blue whales can live 80 years, while mice live only about 2 years. Bats do not follow this rule. Considering their small size, bats live amazingly long lives—most last more than 20 years. The oldest bat on record was a Brandt's bat that scientists had tagged and then recaptured 41 years later.

Peters's epauletted fruit bats are vocal bats, especially as they gather together after a night of foraging.

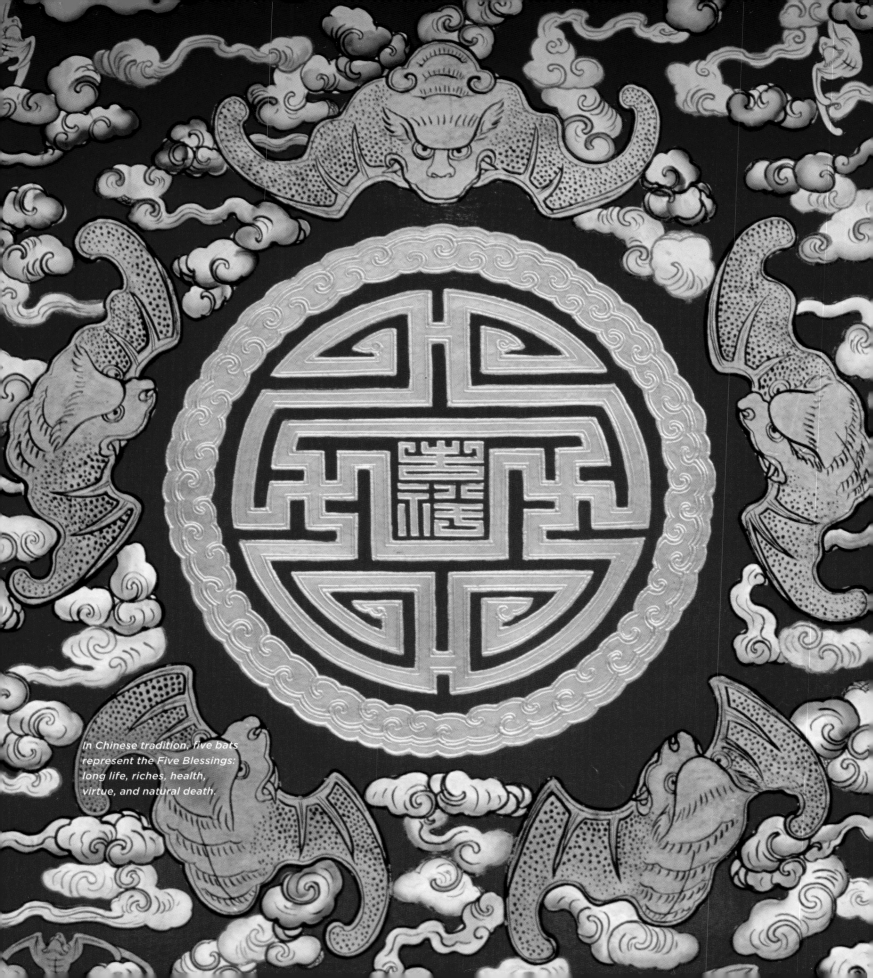

In Chinese tradition, five bats represent the Five Blessings: long life, riches, health, virtue, and natural death.

CREATURES OF THE NIGHT

E quipped with the power of flight and the ability to move swiftly through darkness, bats have traditionally been associated with supernatural beings that possess otherworldly powers. Some cultures feared these creatures of the night, while others respected and even loved them. Ancient tales about bats abound throughout human history.

In ancient Rome, bats were believed to have better natures than humans, since they lived together in large groups and cared for one another. In part of his 12,000-line poem *Metamorphoses*, Ovid tells how the daughters of Minyas (sometimes spelled "Mineus"), a Greek leader, refused to attend an important party. To teach them a lesson, they were turned into bats so they would be forced to remain at home and obey their father.

In the *Popol Vuh*, an ancient Mayan book that comes from the people who once lived in the Central American country of Guatemala, a story is told of batlike monsters that try to kill the heroes, twin brothers who are on an incredible journey. Some scholars believe the creatures were based on the now-extinct giant vampire bat

Long-eared bats' ears can be up to three-quarters the length of their head and bodies.

Fifteen of the nearly 100 species of mouse-eared bat live in North America north of Mexico, but people rarely encounter these shy bats.

species. When the *Popol Vuh* was conceived nearly 3,000 years ago, these bats may have still existed alongside the Mayan people.

Belief in the batlike creatures of the *Popol Vuh* persisted, leading to the emergence, around 100 B.C., of the **cult** of Camazotz among the Zapotec Indians of southern Mexico. Scholars believe that descriptions of this terrifying bat god of the underworld were based on the species called Linnaeus's false vampire bat. This meat-eating bat is known for swooping down on birds, lizards, and other small prey—including other bats—and grabbing the animal's neck to kill it.

Living in areas inhabited by bats led many early people to integrate these creatures into their cultural **mythology**. In the Gran Chaco region of northern Argentina, a country in South America, the Toba people created the story of a heroic bat-man who taught his people how to live as the first human beings. A tribe of Pomo American Indians in California also believed that bats were helpful creatures. They told stories of how bats chewed up chunks of obsidian (a glassy volcanic rock) and then spit out perfectly shaped arrowheads. Some scholars believe this myth was created to explain why the California leaf-nosed bat has arrowhead-shaped nose leaves.

In addition to explaining the relationships between humans and nature, myths may attempt to give reasons for natural occurrences. An Apache myth from a tribe in the American Southwest explains why bats' wings have no fur or feathers. Jonayaiyin, the Sun's child, gave eagle feathers to Bat, but birds would steal the feathers, and Bat would visit Jonayaiyin to ask for more. Eventually, Jonayaiyin told Bat that he could not have any more feathers because he could not take care of them, and Bat's wings have been bare ever since.

Bats are also considered spiritual beings in many cultural myths. Another southwestern tribe, the Navajo, believed that the bat, Jaa'aban, could go places where ordinary people could not go and could carry messages from Talking God, the main Navajo god, to humans. In ancient China, the people thanked bats for eating disease-carrying mosquitoes by including them in images of Shou-Hsing, the god of long life, and in Africa, some people in Uganda and Zimbabwe still believe bats are gentle spirits of the dead. Not all bat spirits are welcome,

Figures of bats have been found in Central American art and architecture dating back to the Mayan culture.

Bram Stoker's visit to England's Whitby Abbey in 1890 inspired him to include this spooky place in his novel Dracula.

however. In Ghana, large fruit bats are feared as demons.

European bat mythology has also traditionally presented bats in a negative light. In the late 18th century, bats became associated with stories of vampires. In the 1750s, French **zoologist** Georges-Louis Leclerc traveled the world to compile his *Histoire Naturelle*, a series of illustrated encyclopedias of natural history. His observations of South American bats that drank blood led him to call these bats "vampires." Writers of popular horror stories in Europe were quick to include vampire bats in their frightening tales.

The myth of the vampire bat not only endured, it grew. In 1897, Irish author Bram Stoker's *Dracula*, perhaps the most famous vampire novel ever written, was published. The horror novel's main character, Count Dracula, could transform himself into a bat, and bats were thereafter linked with vampires. However, not all literary bats have ties to vampires anymore. In British fantasy novelist Robin Jarvis's series The Deptford Mice Trilogy (1989–1990), two bat brothers named Orfeo and Eldritch can foretell the future. Additionally, in Canadian children's author Kenneth Oppel's Silverwing series (1997–2007), a group of

Many Philippine fruit bats roost in caves, but others take shelter in the rainforest trees.

Mexican free-tailed bats may fly nearly 2 miles (3.2 km) high and travel up to 60 miles (97 km) per hour when gliding on wind currents.

Bats need moisture and will sometimes cling to walls in humid areas to keep from dehydrating.

Skilled at climbing along its rocky western U.S. and Mexican habitat, the pallid bat carries its insect prey back to its roost before feeding.

heroic bats embark on a dangerous adventure and exhibit remarkable strength and courage.

Another fictional hero who defies the common stereotypes most often assigned to bats in current popular culture is Batman. First conceived by DC Comics artist Bob Kane and writer Bill Finger in 1939, Batman fights crime without the aid of any superpowers. Masked and costumed with wings like a bat, Batman, also known as the Dark Knight, is silent and swift like a bat. He is also just and compassionate, a solitary figure reminiscent of the ancient mythical bat-creatures that cared for and assisted humans.

Real bats often appear on television and in movies—mostly in tales of terror involving vengeful, blood-sucking bats. But the animals were also valuable to the U.S. government during World War II. In 1943, a top-secret project experimented with "Bat Bombs," which involved attaching tiny bombs to bats, turning the creatures loose in Japanese cities at night, and then detonating the bombs via timers as the bats roosted in buildings during the day. Two million dollars was spent on the project before it was abandoned in favor of further development of the atomic bomb project.

Despite the many connections humans have had with bats, people have long been bats' greatest threat. The need for bat conservation has become more urgent in recent years, as urban development and other human activities influence bat populations. One-quarter of the world's bat species are listed as threatened or endangered on the Red List that is published by the International Union for Conservation of Nature (IUCN).

In cool weather, bats wrap up their wings tightly as they roost, but when it is warm, they fan out their wings.

It may not seem possible, but a bat's toes can remain relaxed while clutching a roosting spot on a cave ceiling.

MYSTERIOUS MAMMALS

Most early bats lived in tropical areas that did not provide ideal conditions for fossil formation, so the earliest bat fossils, which are about 60 million years old, consist only of teeth. However, complete and well-preserved fossils of 50-million-year-old northern bats show that modern bats have survived virtually unchanged for millions of years. It is only in the last century that they have begun to suffer because of human interference. Cavers or tourists can disturb cave-dwelling bats. Bats that live in cities are often intentionally killed or forced out of their dwellings. And logging operations and **deforestation** destroy those bats that live in forests.

The North American Symposium on Bat Research (NASBR) is an organization that brings bat conservation and research groups together from all around the world. One of NASBR's current projects studies the effects of wind energy operations on bats. Huge wind **turbines** that stand 230 feet (70 m) tall are used on large expanses of flat land or the tops of cliffs to harness wind energy. At virtually every site, dead bats have been found on the ground beneath the turbines. Researchers have found

The spotted bat, one of the rarest bats in the world, is black with three white spots and has the largest ears of any North American bat.

Researchers have found that shutting down wind turbines at night can decrease bat fatalities by 70 percent.

that air pressure drops suddenly as the air flows over the turbine blades. When bats fly through these low-pressure areas, their lungs instantly overfill with air, and, like balloons blown up too big, the lungs burst, causing the bats to die of internal bleeding.

Forest-dwelling bats suffer from habitat loss when loggers cut down trees where bats roost. The long-legged myotis is a small, reddish-brown bat that roosts in old trees all along the coast of western North America. Little is known about the habitat needs of these bats, so they are now being studied by the U.S. Forest Service. The long-tailed bat is the subject of another forest study, this one in the Kinleith Pine Plantation on New Zealand's North Island. Such projects will determine how best to manage forests where these threatened bat species live.

Bats are fragile creatures, and special equipment is needed to capture them for biological and behavioral study. Mist nets, which resemble volleyball nets in structure, are often used in bat research. Nearly invisible nylon netting is strung between two poles and placed in the path of bats. Even if a bat's echolocation detects the netting, it often cannot maneuver fast enough to avoid being caught.

THE DAUGHTERS OF MINYAS TRANSFORMED INTO BATS

But Mineus' daughters still their tasks pursue,
To wickedness most obstinately true:
At Bacchus still they laugh, when all around,
Unseen, the timbrels hoarse were heard to sound.
Saffron and myrrh their fragrant odours shed,
And now the present deity they dread.
Strange to relate! Here ivy first was seen,
Along the distaff crept the wond'rous green.
Then sudden-springing vines began to bloom,
And the soft tendrils curl'd around the loom:
While purple clusters, dangling from on high,
Ting'd the wrought purple with a second die.

Now from the skies was shot a doubtful light,
The day declining to the bounds of night.
The fabrick's firm foundations shake all o'er,
False tigers rage, and figur'd lions roar.
Torches, aloft, seem blazing in the air,
And angry flashes of red light'nings glare.
To dark recesses, the dire sight to shun,
Swift the pale sisters in confusion run.
Their arms were lost in pinions, as they fled,
And subtle films each slender limb o'er-spread.
Their alter'd forms their senses soon reveal'd;
Their forms, how alter'd, darkness still conceal'd.
Close to the roof each, wond'ring, upwards springs,
Born on unknown, transparent, plumeless wings.
They strove for words; their little bodies found
No words, but murmur'd in a fainting sound.
In towns, not woods, the sooty bats delight,
And, never, 'til the dusk, begin their flight;
'Til Vesper rises with his ev'ning flame;
From whom the Romans have deriv'd their name.

From Book IV of Metamorphoses,
Ovid (43 B.C.–A.D. 17),
translated by John Dryden (1631–1700)

Some people of the South Pacific islands keep bats as pets—and they also serve roast bat as a delicacy.

Researchers immediately remove the trapped bat so it does not become entangled, which can damage its wings.

To avoid any risk of injuring bats' wings, scientists use a harp trap. A square or rectangular frame supports two parallel walls made up of multiple threads that are strung vertically, resembling a harp, and a bag made of plastic sheeting is attached to the bottom of the frame to catch the bats. The trap is then set up at cave entrances or around tree roosting areas. Using its echolocation, a bat will detect the first wall of threads and swerve to pass between them. But the bat will then collide with the second wall of threads and tumble into the collecting bag.

Scientists can track captured bats by fitting them with Passive Integrated Transponder, or PIT, tags. These tiny electronic capsules are permanently inserted under the skin of a bat's back. The tags transmit information about where and when bats enter or exit their roosts, where they fly, and how fast and far they fly. This information helps conservationists improve efforts to monitor the health and populations of bats.

Not all transmitters are permanent, though. Devices less than half the size of a penny or smaller are attached to bats on a temporary basis. These transmitters send radio signals over long distances, providing scientists with information on roosting and feeding habits. The transmitters are then removed by researchers when bats are caught again, or they self-release after a certain amount of time.

Temporary transmitters are used with great success in the American Southwest to study two endangered bat species, the Mexican long-nosed bat and the lesser long-nosed bat. In the summer, these bats feed on the flowers and fruits of **agaves** and certain cactus species. While feeding, the bats pollinate the plants and disperse seeds. Because they are highly sensitive to environmental disturbances and cannot travel long distances without food, long-nosed bats must roost undisturbed in caves and mines near their food sources. As vital pollinators and seed spreaders, these bats are necessary to the sustained plant growth of their **ecosystem**. Studying the bats, their food sources, and their roosting sites helps scientists find ways to conserve important ecosystems in the southwestern deserts.

Much bat research is also conducted without the use of transmitters. The U.S. Geological Survey (USGS)

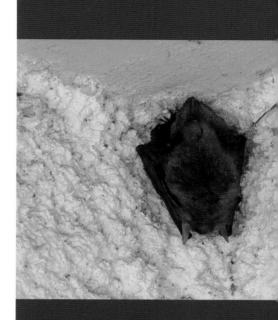

The big brown bat is the only North American bat species capable of surviving through the winter in attics and walls as far north as Canada.

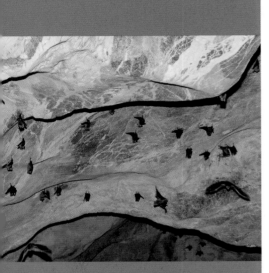

Bat colonies often welcome new members into their fold, which helps increase the variety of mates available.

conducts "fur research" on the migration of several North American bat species that make long-distance seasonal migrations. One bat being studied is the hoary bat, which travels more than 1,240 miles (1,995 km) between seasons. The fur of the bats is examined and compared to weather data in certain locations along their path to determine where bats grow their fur. This knowledge helps scientists track the bats' movements between summer and winter habitats and is used to aid conservation efforts along the bats' migration paths.

Certain types of human interference are subject to much bat research. Humans' use of pesticides and other harmful chemicals in agriculture, their vandalism of roosting areas, responsibility for habitat destruction, extermination of individual bats, and disturbance of bat colonies all contribute to the decline of bat populations around the world. Like any animal species whose natural existence is disturbed, bats are in danger of extinction if their numbers are not properly monitored and managed.

Despite the wealth of new discoveries about the important roles that bats play in their respective

ecosystems, many people still persist in fearing bats. Consequently, these shy creatures have been persecuted and targeted for generations. Continued research and public education may one day dispel the myths surrounding bats and help people better appreciate these fascinating and valuable creatures.

Fruit bats sometimes get tangled in fruit tree netting, fishing line, and barbed wire, putting them at the mercy of humans.

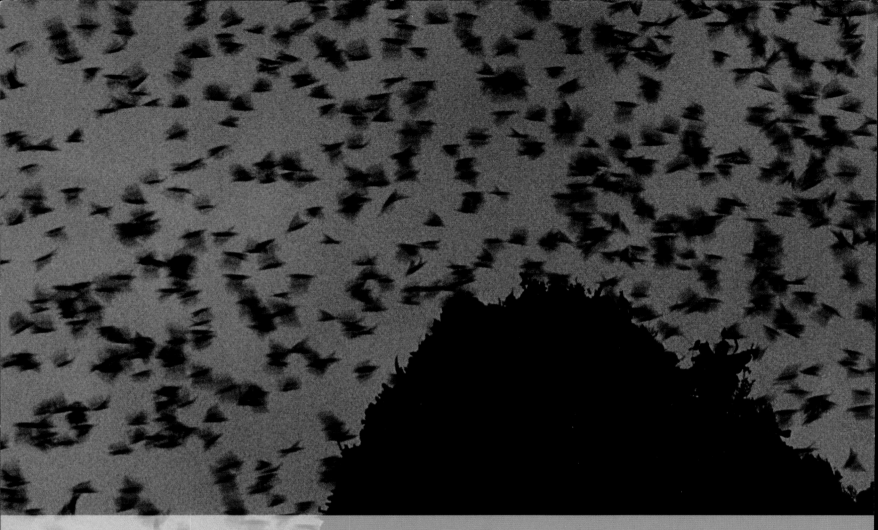

ANIMAL TALE: HOW BAT SHAPED THE EARTH

The bat is one of the most important animals in many American Indian tribes' traditions. Its figure appears in cave drawings, on jewelry and artifacts, and on totems. This ancient Aztec creation story, which has been retold by the people of central Mexico for more than 500 years, tells how the bat helped shape the mountains and valleys of the world in the time of "the ancient people."

When the world began, all the land was flat. When the rain fell, it made all of the land wet and muddy for days and days, and the corn rotted in the fields. The ancient people tried everything they could to shape the land so that crops could be grown, but nothing worked. Rain pounded the earth, and the land stayed flat, and the corn crumbled in the fields and washed away in tatters.

The ancient people called on Lizard and Snake to help. "Please drag your bodies across the land to shape it so our corn will grow," the people asked. Lizard and Snake dragged their bodies all over the land for three days, but they could not change its shape. The land remained flat.

Then the people called on Rabbit, Bear, and Wolf to help. "Please jump, and stomp, and run across the land to shape it so our corn will grow," the people asked. For two days, Rabbit jumped all over the land. Bear stomped all over the land. And Wolf ran all over the land. But they could not change its shape, and the land remained flat.

The people called on all the birds to help.

"Please fly across the land to change its shape so our corn will grow," the people asked. But the birds refused to take on the enormous task. "If neither Lizard nor Snake nor Rabbit nor Bear nor Wolf could shape the land," said Vulture, the chief of all the birds, "we will not be able to shape the land either."

Finally, the people called on Bat. They shouted to the top of a craggy old tree. "Bat, please help us." Bat crept out from beneath the tattered tree bark. He was very old and could barely walk. He crawled down the tree, limping and leaning on a walking stick. His hair was white, and his wings were wrinkled. He told the people he could not help them, but they begged him. "You are our last hope," they said to Bat. So Bat agreed to try to shape the land.

In one night, Bat swooped and darted through the air, flying low to the ground and cutting valleys for the water to run off the fields. But he made the valleys so deep that it became impossible to walk across the land. The chiefs of the ancient people were very unhappy, and they scolded Bat.

"Then I will put the land back as it was before," Bat told the people.

"No, no," said the chiefs. "We just want you to make the valley slopes less steep. Leave some of the land flat, and do not cover it all with mountains."

The next night, Bat did as he was asked, and the chiefs were pleased. They thanked Bat for giving the land the shape they needed to grow corn. And to this day, Earth includes mountains and valleys to keep the rain from settling in the fields and rotting the corn.

GLOSSARY

agaves – tropical American plants with sword-shaped leaves and flowers on tall spikes

camouflaged – hidden, due to coloring or markings that blend in with a given environment

cult – a group of people who worship a particular figure or object

deforestation – the clearing away of trees from a forest

echolocation – a system used by some animals to locate and identify objects by emitting high-pitched sounds that reflect off the object and return to the animal's ears or other sensory organs

ecosystem – a community of organisms that live together in an environment

gestation – the period of time it takes a baby to develop inside its mother's womb

hibernate – to spend the winter in a sleeplike state in which breathing and heart rate slow down

membrane – a thin, clear layer of tissue that covers an internal organ or developing limb

metabolism – the processes that keep a body alive, including making use of food for energy

mythology – a collection of myths, or popular, traditional beliefs or stories that explain how something came to be or that are associated with a person or object

nectar – the sugary fluid produced by a plant

pollen – a powdery material produced by plants and used for reproduction

pollinators – animals or insects that transfer pollen from plant to plant, aiding in plant reproduction

primates – mammals with large brains and gripping hands; lemurs, monkeys, apes, and humans are primates

totems – objects, animals, or plants respected as symbols of a tribe and often used in ceremonies and rituals

turbines – machines that produce energy when wind or water spins through their blades, which are fitted on a wheel or rotor

zoologist – a person who studies animals and their lives

SELECTED BIBLIOGRAPHY

Bat Conservation International. "Homepage." http://www.batcon.org.

Bat World Sanctuary. "Homepage." http://www.batworld.org.

Kunz, Thomas H., and M. Brock Fenton, eds. *Bat Ecology.* Chicago: University of Chicago Press, 2003.

Morrill Allen, Glover. *Bats: Biology, Behavior and Folklore.* Mineola, N.Y.: Dover, 2004.

Nowak, Ronald M. *Walkers' Bats of the World.* Baltimore: Johns Hopkins University Press, 1994.

Tuttle, Merlin D. *America's Neighborhood Bats: Understanding and Learning to Live in Harmony with Them.* Austin: University of Texas Press, 1997.

Bats roost where access is easy and, contrary to what some people believe, never chew a hole to enter a structure.

INDEX